This Notebook Belongs To:

....

Date:

....

Made in the USA
Las Vegas, NV
15 December 2022

62658811R00066